100 QUESTIONS & ANSWERS

NBA Rules & History

Illustrations by Sanford Hoffman
Compiled by Alex Sachare

Sterling Publishing Co., Inc. New York

10 9 8 7 6 5 4 3 2 1

Published by Sterling Publishing Company, Inc.
387 Park Avenue South, New York, N.Y. 10016
© 1996 by NBA Properties, Inc.
Distributed in Canada by Sterling Publishing
%Canadian Manda Group, One Atlantic Avenue, Suite 105
Toronto, Ontario, Canada M6K 3E7
Distributed in Great Britain and Europe by Cassell PLC
Wellington House, 125 Strand, London WC2R 0BB, England
Distributed in Australia by Capricorn Link (Australia) Pty Ltd.
P.O. Box 6651, Baulkham Hills, Business Centre, NSW 2153, Australia
Printed and Bound in France

Sterling ISBN 0-8069-4850-7

How to Use the BipPen

The BipPen must be held straight to point to a black dot.

Point to the black dot.

●

A continuous sound (beeeep) and a red light mean that you've chosen the wrong answer.

Point to the black dot.

●

A discontinuous sound (beep beep beep) and a green light mean that you've chosen the right answer.

Keep your BipPen for other books.

The NBA was formed by owners of arenas in major cities in the eastern half of the United States, many of whom also owned hockey teams, who were looking for some other form of entertainment to draw fans to their buildings and hoped to capitalize on the popularity of college basketball. When was the league formed?

June 6, 1946 ●
June 6, 1937 ■
June 6, 1952 ▲

2

True or false: Basketball players are sometimes known as cagers because the game once was played on a court that was enclosed by a wire mesh cage, to separate the players from the spectators and keep the ball on the court.

True
False ■

3

The diameter of an NBA basket is 18 inches. What is the diameter of an official NBA basketball?

7 inches ●
8 inches ■
9 inches ▲

4

As the abilities of players have grown, there have been modifications in rules and equipment. For example, six inches were taken off the bottom part of the backboard in the 1980s, because there was a fear that players with improved jumping ability would injure themselves by hitting their hands, arms and even heads on the backboard. What are the present dimensions of an NBA backboard?

6 feet by 3 feet ●
6 feet by 3 ½ feet ■
6 feet by 4 feet ▲

5

Teams in the NBA must shoot within a specified period of time or else lose possession of the ball. True or false: This time, which is counted down on a special shot clock, has always been set at 24 seconds.

True
False ■

6

NBA teams may keep either 11 or 12 players on their active rosters. What is the minimum number of players an NBA team must have dressed in uniform and on the bench for a game?

8 ●
9 ■
10 ▲

7

True or false: According to NBA rules, if a shot hits the rim and bounces over the top of the backboard and is then caught by another offensive player who is standing inbounds, the offensive team retains possession.

True ●
False ■

8

Free throws and foul shots are the same thing: uncontested shot attempts awarded to a player when he is fouled, from a line a specific distance from the basket. This free throw line, or foul line, is what distance from the backboard?

12 feet ●
15 feet ■
18 feet ▲

9

In 1979, the NBA began awarding three points for shots made from beyond an arc that was marked on the court. The idea was that by rewarding players for long-range shooting, it would prevent defenses from clogging the middle and enable players to drive to the basket. The distance of that arc from the basket is currently:

19 feet, 9 inches ●
22 feet ■
23 feet, 9 inches ▲

10

True or false: According to NBA rules, for a goaltending violation to occur, a shot must be on its downward arc and must have had, in the official's opinion, a chance at going in had it not been impeded.

True ●
False

Basketball players are always trying to get closer to their goal, the basket. True or false: A player may use a teammate as a springboard to get closer to the basket in order to score.

True
False

If a ball goes out of bounds that is last touched by a player from Team A, possession is awarded to Team B and a player from that team is designated to throw it inbounds. How much time does the player have to inbound the ball before his team loses possession?

3 seconds ●

5 seconds ■

10 seconds ▲

13

If a player who is inbounding the ball lobs it toward the basket and the ball goes directly in, without being touched by another player from either team, what happens?

the basket is nullified and the team
loses possession ●

the basket is nullified but the team
gets to try another throw-in ■

the basket counts ▲

The NBA is headed by a Commissioner, although when the league was first formed the position was entitled President. Who was the first President of the NBA?

Walter Brown
Red Auerbach
Maurice Podoloff

Sometimes the ball can take some strange bounces. True or false: If the ball goes through the basket from below, hits the backboard and then goes through the basket from above, it's a legal basket.

True
False

16

True or false: If a player from either team touches the ball while it is within the imaginary cylinder above the basket ring, it is a goaltending violation against that player's team.

True
False

17

True or false: During the last two minutes of the fourth period or overtime, a team calling a timeout has the option of putting the ball in play from midcourt or from its position when the timeout was called.

True
False

The NBA's Championship Trophy is a depiction of a ball going through a basket, crafted by Tiffany's and given to each title-winning team to keep and display forever. The trophy is named in honor of the man who served from 1975 to 1984 as the NBA's third Commissioner. Who was he?

Bowie Kuhn ●
Pete Rozelle ■
Larry O'Brien ▲

19

True or false: A player who is fouled while attempting a three-point field goal gets to shoot three free throws instead of two, as on other field goal tries.

True
False ■

20

Though it has been called America's Game, basketball was invented by a Canadian, Dr. James Naismith. And the NBA's first game actually was played in this Canadian city.

Montreal ●
Ottawa ■
Toronto ▲

True or false: When a double foul is called, neither team shoots a free throw and the team with the ball retains possession.

True
False ■

Nicknamed "the Big Dipper," this former NBA star averaged 50.4 points per game during the 1961-62 season and scored 100 points in a single game against the New York Knicks. Name him:

Wilt Chamberlain
Elgin Baylor ■
George Mikan ▲

23

Fans usually come to games to cheer on their favorite team or players, but often they boo the opponent as well. True or false: If a fan is excessively abusive toward a player or coach, the game's referees may have him ejected from the arena.

True
False ■

24

The New York Knicks defeated the Toronto Huskies 68-66 in the first game in NBA history. Who scored the league's first basket?

Harry Miller ●
Ossie Schectman ■
Dolph Schayes ▲

A n assist is a pass that leads directly to a basket. What player holds the record for most assists in his NBA career?

John Stockton
Magic Johnson
Oscar Robertson

A lmost all NBA coaches played the game on the college or professional level, and many coached in college or served as assistant coaches before becoming NBA head coaches. What coach has guided his team to more NBA victories than any other?

Red Auerbach
Pat Riley
Lenny Wilkens

True or false: Unlike hockey, where two assists may be awarded on a goal, in basketball only one assist may be given for a successful field goal.

True ●
False ■

How long is a regulation period of an NBA game?

10 minutes ●
12 minutes ■
15 minutes ▲

A triple-double is when a player accumulates double figures in three statistical categories from among points, rebounds, assists, steals and blocked shots. While this feat is relatively rare, one player in NBA history managed to average a triple-double over a full season, compiling double figure averages in points, rebounds and assists. Who was he?

Magic Johnson ●

Wilt Chamberlain ■

Oscar Robertson ▲

How long is the overtime period of an NBA game?

2 minutes ●
until the first
team scores ■
5 minutes ▲

NBA games often include halftime entertainment to keep fans happy while the players are resting. What is the standard amount of time between halves of an NBA game?

10 minutes ●
15 minutes ■
20 minutes ▲

A three-second violation occurs when an offensive player lingers in the free throw lane for more than three seconds. True or false: If a player has one foot in the lane and one foot out, he will not be called for a three-second violation no matter how long he remains that way.

True
False

This franchise has won more NBA Championships than any other, 16. What team is it?

New York
    Knickerbockers
Boston Celtics
Los Angeles Lakers ▲

True or false: The NBA's Boston Celtics competed during the 1920s and 1930s, when they were known as the Original Celtics.

True
False ■

The rim is the metal ring that is attached to the backboard and from which the basketball net is hung. How high off the ground is an NBA rim?

10 feet ●
12 feet ■
15 feet ▲

Officiating is one of the most important, yet most often overlooked, jobs in the NBA. Good officials keep the game moving smoothly and allow the players to play the game at its highest level, providing the best entertainment for fans. In what season did the NBA begin using three officials per game, instead of two?

1988-89 ●
1989-90 ■
1990-91

37

If a player kicks a ball intentionally, it is a violation and the other team gets possession and a new 24 seconds on the shot clock. True or false: If the kick was unintentional, play continues without interruption and there is no violation.

True
False ■

38

True or false: When a free throw is being shot, any player may enter the lane and pursue the rebound as soon as the ball leaves the shooter's hand, but the shooter must remain behind the free throw line until the ball hits the rim.

True
False ■

A basketball court is divided in half by a midcourt line. How much time is an offensive team given to move the ball over the midcourt line before a violation is called?

5 seconds ●
10 seconds ■
no limit ▲

When the NBA was formed, the foul lane was six feet wide. It was later widened to 12 feet and then widened again to its current dimension. How wide is the lane today?

15 feet ●
16 feet ■
18 feet ▲

To give players a chance to rest or allow coaches an opportunity to discuss strategy with their players, teams are permitted a certain number of timeouts during a game. How many (do not include special 20-second timeouts, of which each team receives one per half) timeouts does each team receive?

5 ●
6 ■
7 ▲

Officials must check the balls to be used in each game to see that they are properly inflated. The pressure to which NBA game balls must be inflated is:

between $7\frac{1}{2}$ and $8\frac{1}{2}$ pounds ●
between 8 and 9 pounds ■
between $8\frac{1}{2}$ and $9\frac{1}{2}$ pounds ▲

Thue or false: There is an NBA rule pro-
hibiting the wearing of any type of
hand, arm, face, nose, ear, head or neck
jewelry during a game.

True
False

Two players are battling for a loose ball and it goes out of bounds. One official sees it as going off the player from Team A, while a second official sees it as going off the player from Team B. If the third official does not see the play, what happens?

the team which originally had the ball retains possession ●

there is a jump ball ■

the teams alternate such disputed possessions ▲

If a player becomes ill or injured while the game is going on, when can he be replaced?

immediately ●

as soon as the referee notices the ill or injured player ■

as soon as his team gains possession of the ball ▲

In order to keep the game under control, rulesmakers set a limit on the number of fouls a player may commit before he is disqualified. How many personal fouls is a player permitted before he must leave the game?

5 ●
6 ■
7 ▲

Each team must have five players on the court at a given time. If a player on the court fouls out, and all players on the bench have already fouled out, what happens?

> he is replaced by the last player to be disqualified, and a techincal foul is assessed ●
>
> he remains in the game and a technical foul is assessed ■
>
> he is disqualified and his team must finish the game with only four players. ▲

NBA games are generally played in indoor arenas designed to suit basketball, hockey and other events. Occasionally, however, NBA teams have played in large multi-purpose arenas that also are home to baseball or football teams. The Detroit Pistons, for example, played their home games at the Silverdome for several seasons, where they set the all-time single-game attendance record in 1988. What is the largest crowd ever to watch an NBA game?

49,551 ●
52,745 ■
61,983 ▲

Who was the highest scoring player in the highest scoring game in NBA history—Detroit's 186-184 triple overtime victory over Denver on December 13, 1983?

Isiah Thomas ●
Kelly Tripucka ■
Kiki Vandeweghe ▲

Eleven teams competed in the NBA in its first season, when it was formed as the Basketball Association of America. Which of these cities did not have a team in the original NBA, in 1946-47?

Philadelphia ●
Chicago ■
Baltimore ▲

Who was the first player in NBA history to score 2,000 points in one season?

George Mikan
George Yardley
Bob Pettit

Occasionally, NBA franchises have moved from one city to another for economic reasons. What city did the Sacramento Kings originally call home?

Rochester, NY
Syracuse, NY
Buffalo, NY

Which of the following teams was not an original member of the NBA?

Minneapolis Lakers
St. Louis Bombers
Pittsburgh Ironmen

A zone defense is when a player guards an area of the floor, rather than a specific man. They are permitted at most levels of basketball competition, but are zone defenses permitted in the NBA?

Yes
No

True or false: Although the Coach of the Year receives the Red Auerbach Trophy, Auerbach never won the award himself.

True
False

What team won the first NBA Championship?

Boston Celtics
Philadelphia Warriors
Syracuse Nationals

Who made the first three-point field goal in NBA history?

Larry Bird ●
Chris Ford ■
Craig Hodges ▲

In what season did the NBA institute the 24-second shot clock, which gives teams 24 seconds in which to get off a shot or else lose possession of the ball?

1946-47 ●
1954-55 ■
1961-62 ▲

NBA teams play as many as four or five games in a week, with half their schedule away from home. With the fatigue that comes from repeated travel, long winning streaks are rare—but one team once won 33 games in a row! What team holds the longest consecutive-game winning streak in NBA history?

1963-64 Boston Celtics ●
1946-47 Sheboygan Redskins ■
1971-72 Los Angeles Lakers ▲

60

Teams receive their nicknames in many ways. Some are the result of contests conducted among their fans, while others are chosen by team executives to convey a certain image. True or false: The Detroit Pistons got their nickname because their original owner ran a company that produced pistons for engines.

True
False

61

Before they moved to Los Angeles, the Lakers were based in what city?

Milwaukee
Minneapolis
St. Louis

Before they moved to the San Francisco Bay area, the Golden State Warriors played in what city?

Philadelphia
Syracuse
Rochester

Before they moved to Salt Lake City, Utah, the Jazz were located in what city which is well known for its musical heritage?

Memphis
New Orleans
Nashville

Prior to the Pacers, two other NBA teams called Indianapolis their home. What were their nicknames?

Hoosiers and Indians
Hoosiers and Olympians
Jets and Olympians

"Ironmen" is the nickname of one of the NBA's original franchises, although the team survived for only the inaugural 1946-47 season before folding. In what city did the Ironmen play?

Altoona, PA
Pittsburgh, PA
Harrisburg, PA

In 1977, this team won its only NBA Championship in its first appearance in the playoffs. Led by Bill Walton and Maurice Lucas, what team was it?

Portland Trail Blazers
Sacramento Kings
San Diego Clippers

The American Basketball Association competed for nine seasons, from 1967-68 through 1975-76. Then, four teams from the ABA joined the NBA to bring the number of teams in the league to 22. Which of the following teams did not join the NBA from the ABA?

Dallas Mavericks
San Antonio Spurs
Indiana Pacers

68

In 1986, this team won 40 home games and lost only 1 for the best home record in NBA history. What team was it?

Los Angeles Lakers
Boston Celtics
Chicago Bulls

69

Many say that repeating as champion is even more difficult than winning a title for the first time. What was the first NBA team to win back-to-back titles?

Minneapolis Lakers
Boston Celtics
Philadelphia Warriors

Which team celebrated the early 1970s with two titles in four years—its only championships since it entered the NBA as a charter member in 1946-47?

Washington Bullets
New York Knicks ■
St. Louis Bombers ▲

Which team won its only NBA title in 1978, when its coach, Dick Motta, adopted as the club's never-say-die motto: "The opera isn't over till the fat lady sings"?

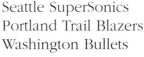

Seattle SuperSonics
Portland Trail Blazers
Washington Bullets ▲

Which of the following players did not win Most Valuable Player and Rookie of the Year honors in the same season?

Michael Jordan
Wilt Chamberlain ■
Wes Unseld ▲

In the NBA's first season, this player averaged 23.2 points per game while the second-leading scorer in the league averaged just 16.8 ppg. Who was the first scoring champion in NBA history?

George Mikan
Bob Cousy ■
Joe Fulks ▲

Who is the only player in NBA history to be the Most Valuable Player of the NBA Finals while playing on the losing team?

Magic Johnson, LA Lakers in
1986   ●
Jerry West, LA Lakers in 1969 ■
Wilt Chamberlain, LA Lakers
in 1973   ▲

Who was the first player in NBA history to lead the league in field goal percentage by shooting better than 50 percent for the season?

Neil Johnston in 1952-53   ●
Wilt Chamberlain in 1960-61   ■
Jerry Lucas in 1963-64   ▲

Which of the following men did not win Coach of the Year honors in both the NBA and the ABA?

Tom Nissalke
Alex Hannum ■
Larry Brown ▲

A good shotblocker is the anchor of any team's defense, keeping opponents away from the basket and forcing them to take more difficult shots. Who is the only man in NBA history to lead the league in blocked shots four times within a five-year span?

Mark Eaton
Kareem Abdul-Jabbar ■
Hakeem Olajuwon ▲

Basketball can be played on a court of virtually any shape and size, as long as you have at least one basket for a target. According to the official rule book, however, what is the optimum size of an NBA court?

50 feet by 100 feet ●
50 feet by 94 feet ■
54 feet by 100 feet ▲

Basketball is such a fast-paced sport that often several things take place at the same time. What happens, for example, if one referee calls a foul and another calls a violation at the same time?

the foul takes precedence ●
the violation takes precedence ■
a jump ball is called ▲

Sometimes, by accident, a player will shoot the ball into the wrong basket. It doesn't happen very often, and usually it occurs when several players are trying to grab or tip a rebound. What is the official rule if Player A tips the ball into Team B's goal?

the basket is nullified but Team B gets possession ●

the basket goes to Team B and is credited to its player nearest Player A ■

the basket goes to Team A even though it went through the wrong basket ▲

An NBA team may have a designated captain or co-captains numbering a maximum of two. True or false: According to the rule book, the designated captain is the only player who may talk to the referees during a timeout.

True ●
False ■

If a player is ejected from a game because of unsportsmanlike conduct, he may watch the remainder of the game:

from the team bench ●
from any part of the
    arena except the
      team bench area ■
on television only ▲

Can you tell a player without a scorecard? For many years, a player's uniform only listed the team name or nickname and the player's number, but in recent years, teams began listing the player's name as well. True or false: NBA teams now are required to put players' names on the backs of their jerseys.

True ●

False ■

If the ball happens to hit the back of the backboard, it is considered out of play. But what happens if it hits the top, bottom or sides of the backboard?

in play in all cases ●

out of play in all cases ■

out of play for the top,
in play otherwise ▲

A player attempting a free throw must do so within a specific amount of time after receiving the ball from the referee, or else he forfeits his attempt. How much time does a player have in which to shoot?

5 seconds
10 seconds ■
15 seconds ▲

True or false: A player who keeps one foot planted on the floor may take as many steps as he wants with the other foot, in as many directions as he wants, as long as he does not pick up the first (or "pivot") foot.

True ●
False

87

A player must have both feet behind the three-point arc in order to be credited with a three-point field goal. If even one foot is touching the line, it's a two-pointer. But how many points is the basket worth if the player takes off with both feet behind the line, but comes down on or inside the line?

2 points
3 points

88

When a player commits his sixth personal foul, he is disqualified from the game and must be replaced in the lineup. How long does a coach have to decide on a replacement?

30 seconds
one minute
a "reasonable"
    amount of
    time

Each team is entitled to call seven regular timeouts per game, and one 20-second timeout per half. What happens if a team has used its allotment of timeouts and requests another?

the official ignores the request and play continues ●

the official grants the timeout but assesses a technical foul against the team that called it ■

the official grants the timeout but takes away possession of the ball ▲

A team must attempt a shot within 24 seconds of gaining possession of the ball, or else it loses the ball to the other team. What happens if a shot is attempted but it fails to hit the basket?

the 24-second clock is reset ●
play continues ■
play is stopped and the other
   team gets the ball ▲

If a team has possession of the ball and it goes out of bounds, off a player from the defensive team, with just one second remaining on the 24-second shot clock, what happens?

the 24-second clock is reset to 10 ●
the 24-second clock is reset to 5 ■
the 24-second clock remains at 1 ▲

Team A is given possession of the ball under its own basket. A long throw-in is attempted, but the ball bounces out of bounds at the far end of the court without being touched by any player from either team. Who gets the ball, and where?

Team B, at the point where the throw-in was attempted ●

Team B, at the point where the ball went out of bounds ■

Team A, at the point where the throw-in was attempted ▲

If a player from Team A is injured while being fouled and unable to shoot the free throws he is awarded on the play, he is removed from the game and is not permitted to reenter the game at a later time. But who determines who shoots the free throws?

the coach of Team B selects a player to shoot, from among Team A's other players in the game at the time ●

the coach of Team B selects a player to shoot, from among the players on Team A's bench at the time ■

the coach of Team A selects a player to shoot, from among the players on Team A's bench at the time ▲

94

Before its name was changed to National Basketball Association in 1949, the league was known by what name?

National Basketball Alliance
Basketball Association of America
National Basketball League ▲

95

If a player takes two steps without dribbling the ball, a traveling violation is called and the other team receives possession of the ball. True or false: If a player falls down and slides along the floor while in possession of the ball, a traveling violation may be called and his team will lose possession.

True ●
False ■

Once a team moves the ball over the midcourt line into its frontcourt, it may not take the ball into the backcourt again. If that happens, a backcourt violation is called and the other team takes possession at midcourt. Would it be a backcourt violation if a player takes off from the backcourt, catches a pass that originated in the frontcourt in mid-air and lands in the frontcourt?

Yes ●
No ■

If a player, in jumping to retrieve an errant shot, holds onto the backboard with one hand and tips the ball into the basket with the other, is it considered a legal basket?

Yes

No ■

It is considered a goaltending violation if Player A traps the ball against the backboard. What happens if Player A bats the ball against the backboard while it is still on its upward flight?

no violation, play continues ●

goaltending, team B gains
    possession ■

jump ball ▲

A screen is when one player assumes a stationary position and a teammate cuts closely by him in an attempt to free himself from his defender, by brushing the defender off on the screening player. It is a legal and important part of team basketball play. What happens if, in running a play along the baseline, a player sets a screen with one foot out of bounds, beyond the baseline?

it is a legal screen and play continues ●

it is an illegal screen and his team loses possession of the ball ■

it is an illegal screen and the opposing team receives a free throw ▲

Player A attempts a shot that is so far off target that it touches neither rim nor basket nor backboard. No player is in position for the rebound, the before the ball hits the ground, Player A races over and recovers it before it is touched by another player from either team. What happens?

play continues ●

play continues, but the 24-second clock is reset ■

it is considered a traveling violation and Team B gains possession ▲